Over the Rainbow

Over the Rainbow

Memoir of a Kansas Girl

MARY ERLANGER

INTERVIEW
You

ATHENS, GEORGIA

Published by Interview You,
an imprint of Miglior Press

Athens, Georgia

www.interviewyou.net

The text of this book is set in ITC Legacy Serif,
designed by Ronald Arnholm.

Cover design by The Adsmith

ISBN 978-0-9822726-4-0

First Edition

Printed in the United States of America

To my grandchildren—Katie, Caroline, and Aaron—
who have brought me so much joy—and
to my first great-grandchild,
Thomas Ray Askew, born August 22, 2013

Do what you can, want what you have, be who you are.

—Forrest Church

Contents

Preface

Like many of my peers, I have often thought about writing my life story. The times have been extraordinary and the experiences richly rewarding, and I wanted to leave a record for my descendants. Of course, I never got around to it.

Only with the encouragement, organization, and skilled help from my friends Donna Maddock-Cowart and David Cowart and my granddaughter Katie Folkman has this narrative come to fruition. They conducted and edited numerous interviews and worked with my collection of photographs to help me develop this memoir. I am so grateful for their support and perseverance in putting this all together.

I am also deeply grateful for my long life. It has been rich with adventures, education, challenging jobs, wonderful friendships, and a loving marriage and family. I honestly do feel that I have been "over the rainbow."

Mary Erlanger

Where my father grew up: the Fears Plantation in Hampton, Georgia

Family History

I was born in Manhattan, Kansas, in July of 1922, not long after my father arrived there as a minister. I lived in Manhattan until I graduated from Kansas State College at the age of twenty, and it will always be my "hometown." However, we had no family connection there.

My father's father, a doctor in Tennessee, died shortly after my father was born. A few years later, my grandmother married Grady Fears and moved to Hampton, Georgia, where my father, J. David Arnold, grew up on their peach plantation. Eventually, there were several half-siblings. They all grew up in the old Fears place, which now exists as a bed and breakfast. My father wanted to be a doctor like his father, but the only college he could afford to attend was a Bible college not too far away. While he was there, he got a tennis scholarship to Drake University, where he got a ministerial degree and began a career as a minister. Around 1914, he was called to Fort Smith, Arkansas, where he met and married my mother, Louise Boone.

Mother's great-grandfather was related to Daniel Boone's brother, Squire Boone. A branch of the family moved to Oxford, Mississippi, where my maternal grandfather, Thomas William Miles Boone, grew up. When my grandfather was three years old, his father was killed in the Civil War. When he was seventeen, he and his mother, along with a servant who was probably a freed slave, set

out for the frontier, where they had some family connections, to make a new life. When they arrived in Fort Smith,
Arkansas, which was still very much pioneer territory, my
grandfather taught school and read law at night (just as
Abraham Lincoln had).

T. W. M. Boone met Ella McBride, a fellow teacher, who
had come from Missouri to teach, surely an adventure at
that time. The two teachers met and married and had four
children. The three Boone girls—my mother, Louise, and
my aunts, Nell and Margaret—were fairly close in age and
stayed close their entire lives. Their brother, Miles, became
estranged from the family when he was a young man, rec-
onciling many years later.

My grandfather had a very successful career as an at-
torney and banker. My mother grew up in a beautiful
home in Fort Smith; the family also had a summer home,
at Winslow in the Ozarks. For the first seven years of my
life, my mother, my sister, and I would take the train to
Arkansas to spend the summers with all the aunts and
cousins. Winslow was a beautiful place—a typical Ozarks
retreat in the mountains. There was a huge veranda going
all the way around, with lots of rocking chairs. The house
was big and comfortable, with a few servants to cook and
take care of everything. Outside, we had a tennis court and
a croquet court and chickens roaming about—including
a scary rooster named Thomas Jefferson. We spent a lot
of time playing games and listening to the old Victrola,
through which the Italian tenor Enrico Caruso would en-
tertain us in the evenings.

My grandparents' summer home in Winslow, Arkansas

A summer photo from Winslow: I was about three years old.

Everything changed in 1929 when the crash devastated my grandparents' finances. My grandfather's bank—he was president of the bank—failed, and one of his partners absconded with funds. My grandfather, being such an honorable man, sold everything to pay off the bank depositors.

During what would be our last visit to Winslow, I celebrated my seventh birthday. After that summer, things were to be very different. My grandparents had to sell their big house in Fort Smith and move to a cottage that my grandfather had been managing as a real-estate investment. My grandmother, who was the quintessential Southern lady, had a hard time with the transition. I remember her taking to her bed and becoming a semi-invalid from then on. She had likely suffered a heart attack, given that permanent bed rest was the most common prescription for heart problems in those days. She died about ten years later: she was a reader, and she left every one of her grandchildren a complete set of Charles Dickens. "Mamama," as we called her, was an imposing character, though I must say that most of my impressions of my grandmother are from my mother's stories. She was always supervising, my mother told me, a quality that my mother shared to some extent. Manners were very important to my grandmother, as was conformity. I remember not being able to chew gum in her presence. For Mamama, good manners and proper behavior were part of being an educated woman, and education was the most important thing a woman could have.

When the Winslow summers had to end, we began visiting my father's family in Georgia every other year. It was quite something in the early '30s to drive all the way from Kansas to Georgia. It was an adventure for all of us, and it was fun. To make the time pass, we would sing and play a counting game regarding various objects or animals, and read and recite the limericks on the famous Burma Shave signs.

When we were hungry, we would stop at roadside stands and buy peaches or bunches of grapes to eat. Real meals, and places to stay, were more complicated to find. When we were ready to stop, we would look for signs on the houses we were passing, signs announcing that tourists were "accommodated." When we found one, we would pull over, and Mother would go in first to make sure the place was suitable. By the standards of today's hotels and motels, they were primitive places with modest sleeping facilities and simple, family-style meals.

We would stop in Fort Smith and stay with my mother's sister, Aunt Nell. She had four children, all a little older than me. Of course, we would also visit the grandparents, and then we would leave for Georgia. Aunt Margaret and her family lived in Atlanta, which I loved. It was the only city we visited on those trips, and we would go to the Fox Theater (so exciting!) and Rich's fabulous department store. After Atlanta, we would visit my father's family. He had half-brothers and sisters, some of whom we would visit along the way, but our destination was always Granny Fears in Hampton, Georgia.

Granny Fears, my father's mother, lived on her own plantation, in a big red brick house with columns, a typical pre-Civil War southern home. She was widowed early in her second marriage; she continued to run the plantation as a widow for many years. (I always respected that both my grandmothers were women who lived very independent and productive lives at a time when that would not have been easy.) When we went to visit Granny Fears, people would come around to see us, and we would sit outside, eat watermelon out on the porch, and have seed-spitting contests with our cousins. We ate fried chicken and okra, a special favorite of mine.

Those summer trips were our connection to both my mother's and father's families; we had no relatives in Kansas. The trips were important to my parents as both of them had a strong sense of family and were eager to maintain those connections. Throughout her life, my mother kept up regular correspondence with her father and looked forward to his letters, as I'm sure he looked forward to hers.

While we were far from relatives in Kansas, we were hardly alone. The members of the church—the First Christian Church of Manhattan, Kansas—where my father was minister, made up our extended family, and we felt deeply connected to this warm community of people. It was a sizable downtown church, a congregational church which called its own minister. The congregation had called my father to come to Manhattan around 1920, and he stayed

with that church until he retired around 1960. After re-
tiring, he did ad-interim ministries all over the country,
but Manhattan was really always their home—and my
hometown.

The Independent Childhood of a
Kansas Minister's Daughter

I grew up in the "parsonage," a gathering place for many church meetings and associations. It was fairly spacious, with a front porch, a yard for playing, bedrooms upstairs and down, and a study for my father. In the early years I shared a room with my sister, but for most of them I had my own room, which I treasured.

The parsonage in Manhattan, Kansas

My sister, Louise, who was four years older than me, was an important part of my life. On a trip to visit my father's family in Georgia when she was an infant, she became seriously ill with what may have been meningitis. She had a high fever for days, which affected her brain, and she never developed a normal IQ. Of course, this was a major factor for my family when I was growing up. In my early childhood we made many trips to the Menninger Clinic in Topeka, seeking a diagnosis and help. Louise required a lot of focus and attention from my mother—and I probably asked for a lot of attention, too! So when I turned four, Mother took me to the school, had me tested, and I was admitted to kindergarten.

I went to Woodrow Wilson School, which was just across the street and half a block away from our house. I always liked school and got good grades, except for "talks too much." I had some pretty good teachers, and Mother was a born teacher herself. She taught me to read when I was quite young. I remember in first grade, when I was five, standing in front of the class and reading a story to everyone. From then on, I was always a reader. The public library was close to where we lived; I could walk there by myself from the time I was six, cutting across the school-yard. I loved that library, and going by myself was a great treat. I was not allowed into the adult section, but I could go to the children's section and get whatever books I wanted to bring home. In seventh grade I started junior high school, which was also in walking distance, and I was still able to go home for lunch every day.

For all those years growing up, it was almost always three meals a day together, with the whole family at the table. My father was helpful—he would go buy the groceries—but Mother was unquestionably the cook, and she was such a good cook! I remember one specialty most fondly: her yeast rolls. They would have to rise, part of their appeal, and then the smell of baking filled the house. Our everyday meals were largely Southern cooking: fried chicken, pot roast, ham and grits, sweet potatoes, and collard greens. Those were my father's favorites, the dishes he had grown up eating. The black population in Manhattan at the time was not large, but there were a couple of black preachers who really connected with my father. They would come around to bring us black-eyed peas and collard greens, a real treat for him.

§

I remember my father having his own shortwave radio and listening as Lindbergh flew across the ocean in '27. Very soon after that, we had a console radio in our living room to listen to the news and a program on Sunday afternoon, a classic called *Our Gal Friday*. Then we began to listen to comedians like Fred Allen and Jack Benny. I always loved to laugh, and so I remember those early radio shows very well. For other entertainment, people were usually stopping by to visit, and in the evenings, we could sit on the front porch. There were so many evenings of children playing all around, and people walking by and visiting.

There were playmates in the neighborhood then, so I could just go outside and play with the neighbors. Also, there were plenty of things for kids to do in town. In the summer, we went to a big park with a huge, round swimming pool. That pool was the focus of summer. At a certain age, I could walk there by myself and so going to the pool became my summer entertainment. Believe me, in those hot Kansas summers, it was a godsend! Summer weather was extreme in Kansas. For years we had a terrible drought, filled with grasshoppers and dust and sun and heat. My father moved his study to the basement, and Louise and I slept on the dining room floor with damp sheets to survive the hot nights.

§

It was the '30s, and the times were so bad. There was a lot of poverty in that era by any standard. The farmers were suffering the most. The state had to cut the professors' salaries in half during that time, and I'm sure the same thing happened to my father's salary. During that time, we kept a little garden out of necessity, and we had chickens for a while. There would be transient people who came to our back door asking for food, and Mother would always find a plate of food for them. I'm sure there was some code for passing the word because we had many backdoor visitors.

§

Thanksgiving was a holiday when we invited people over who did not have anywhere else to go, mostly the elderly and college students. Christmas was more about family, but it was very church-involved, too. There was always a Christmas Eve service at the church that everybody would attend. One member of the congregation who was rather plump and had a white beard would be Santa Claus. He would have treats for all the children, and I loved him! We also had a Christmas tree. We decorated it with lights, but we just had paper decorations for the rest. Despite the Depression, there were always presents of some sort. On Christmas morning, Louise and I would go downstairs and be surprised by it all, then open our very simple presents. My favorite memory is of getting a "sugar baby" doll once that I really loved.

Easter was then a major church event, and also the holiday for fashion. Mother always got a new hat for Easter. Mother did love clothes, especially hats, although she could rarely shop because of the financial situation. However, through all those Depression years my father did a lot of weddings; these were especially important to my family because they were a source of extra income. Of course, the fees were voluntary, and they were probably five or ten dollars, at most. Mother got the fees from the weddings and funerals; that money was her separate little treasure fund, which she would use to buy a dress or a hat. Spending thousands of dollars on a wedding just was not a possibility in those days, so there were very few big church weddings. The couples would simply go to the church or, more often, they came to our house. With my mother acting as director of the student program at the church and Manhattan being a college town, there were a lot of students getting married at our house. The wedding party would usually include the couple, with maybe two friends or parents. Our living room was the site of the wedding ceremony. I was fascinated by it all, and I would be on the staircase peeping through the railings of the banister to watch.

§

I had a lot of independence. Mother was very focused on seeing that Louise's life was as good as it could be. So as long as I was getting good grades and not having any behavior problems, I was very much on my own for those years. Late in life, when I started really studying psychology, I came across the principle of "benign neglect." That principle fits so well with my upbringing; I feel I really benefited from having the nurturing I needed, but being able to manage my own life. Louise, meanwhile, was in the public schools until I caught up with her in the fourth grade; then mother helped start a "special room" at the junior high school for what we now call "special-needs" children. The school hired a designated teacher for that group, and Louise spent a number of years there. In the end, she could read and write and play the piano. Louise was a very talented musician, actually, and a very sweet person. My parents did not ask me to take responsibility for her.

I loved my bicycle (circa 1938)

With my mohter, father, and sister Louise in our living room, 1938

There was a minimum of conflict and stress in our house. My father was very supportive of my mother, and she of him. They had a good time together, and our household was filled with good humor. I do remember when I started "talking back" as a teenager—they did not like that at all.

My father and I always had a very warm relationship. He was accepting and loving. Mother's approval was much harder to get. I can still picture her glare from across the room after I said a naughty word like "darn," or did something else that was not acceptable. It was clear that she was always trying very hard to bring me up properly.

With my sister, I had a much more "removed" relationship. I felt a lot of responsibility and a certain amount of guilt for not wanting to include her in my life and activities. It was also hard for the two of us to have our own interactions because Mother was always with her. Overall, I am grateful to my parents for my upbringing. They were both very loving and really wonderful people.

My father, the Rev. J. David Arnold   *My mother, Louise Boone Arnold*

§

My parents also looked for activities that would help me to develop and evolve. I took piano lessons, but I was not very good at piano. My sister was much better. Then I took violin, and I am sure I was terrible. That was in junior high, and I played in the school orchestra. I can still see the look on my father's face when he heard me practicing—I think his reaction encouraged me to give it up. We had a neighbor who taught elocution, so I took elocution lessons when I was about ten. She also had a little drama group, and I appeared in some theatrical performances under her direction and loved it.

I really loved the movies as a child. There again, money was a factor, but my father was appointed to the Board of Censors in Manhattan (local censoring existed at the time), which meant that he had free passes to the movies. So, I went to a lot of movies that I would not have gone to otherwise. Those films were carefully selected, of course. Early on, the big treat on Saturday mornings was going to a theater where they had Tarzan serials and Mickey Mouse cartoons. The Saturday shows were shorts for children; it cost about ten cents to get in. I remember going to see Laurel and Hardy, and early Charlie Chaplin films, *The Jazz Singer* with Al Jolson, then later, of course, *Gone with the Wind*. I used to save pictures of Joan Crawford, Clark Gable, Loretta Young, and various other movie stars who were the icons of the time.

I did not begin going to the movies alone with my friends until junior high school when I was eleven. Junior high school was when I really remember beginning to develop my own little clique of friends and doing things with them. Then during high school, three of my friends and I had a play-reading club that would meet on Saturdays. We would get the Burns Mantle collection of *Best Plays* (an annual publication) from the library, and we would assign parts and read those plays aloud. One girl in that group, Dorothy Summers, became one of my lifelong friends. Her father was a professor of radio communication, and we were both smitten with the idea of going to New York. While we were in high school, she and I would meet on Saturdays, dressed in whatever finery we could find in our closets, and go downtown and pretend we were going to New York. Those downtown excursions came to an end when her family really did move to New York, but I did not let go of the idea.

I had New York City on my mind, even then. Movies like *Gold Diggers of 1933* mesmerized me. The movies were all about dancing and music in New York. Seeing those made me realize I liked that energy and wanted to be a part of it. I made a promise to myself that, someday, I would go to New York.

A Soapbox and a Defining Moment

In high school, I always liked reading and writing. I worked on our high school paper and was very involved in it; that experience, I am sure, led me to focus on journalism as a career. It was during those high school years that my life as political junkie also began. This happened in the time of the Spanish Revolution. I had a sociology teacher who was really inspiring, but he must have been very left wing because I got interested in combating fascism. In fact, a friend and I even decided to join the Communist Party! So we wrote to them, applying for membership; they wrote back to say they would not accept us. The reason, of course, was that we were only fifteen. I was not entirely deterred. On senior-class day, when we all came dressed as something that represented our aspirations, I wore a red shirt and carried a soapbox. Despite the times, they did not attack me or throw me out of school. My father, meanwhile, was very much a staunch Roosevelt Democrat. I grew up with those values, whereas Kansas was quite definitely conservative Republican, although not at all to the extent that it is now.

When I was finishing high school and getting ready for college, my father ran for mayor of Manhattan and won. I think he did it largely to earn some extra money so that I could go to college. Of course, I would still have to go to college in town; going away was not really an option.

For being mayor, my father received a modest stipend, and that really did see me through the college years. He was mayor for two terms. There were some church members who did not think it was totally appropriate for their minister to serve as mayor of the town, so he quit after his second term. I know he loved the job, though, because he loved people and thrived with being in the thick of things and making decisions. People loved him, too. When I was back in Manhattan for his funeral in 1963, I remember meeting somebody on the street who said, "You know, the one thing that I remember about your father is that I never heard anybody say anything bad about him."

§

I lived at home through college, but I also joined a sorority. Five of my good friends and I pledged the same sorority, Pi Beta Phi, and so I would go to the sorority house to smoke cigarettes and hang out with my friends.

Then I got involved in the college paper, and it became a major focus in my life. I was getting a journalism degree, and I was always working on the paper. In the summers, I would work on the local newspaper in Manhattan. When I was a junior in 1941, I became editor of the weekly college paper. In that capacity, I was writing all kinds of pacifist editorials about how war is evil and how we should stay out of the conflict in Europe.

Outside the Pi Phi sorority house, I am with my close friends Betty Ann Faubion and Audrey Durland.

I am with fellow journalist Marjorie Rogers at Kansas State.

Then one day, a single event put in motion sweeping change that would affect the country, the world, and, of course, my own life. I had gone to the sorority house for a Sunday midday dinner. It was a typical Sunday in that I would usually get home from church with my parents and then take the family car to have dinner at the Pi Phi house. That day, driving home on December 7, 1941, I heard the broadcast: Pearl Harbor had been attacked. I still get choked up and feel goose bumps when I think about those moments. It was incredibly powerful. I went straight home and wrote my editorial saying: *We have to win. We have no choice. We have to defend ourselves and so let's do it.*

We had a big ROTC unit on the campus. By the time I graduated, a year and a half after Pearl Harbor, there were no men on the campus at all; it was total immersion in the war and no divisiveness about it. Our campus had its own personal connections to the effort. For one, Fort Riley, home of the ninth armored division, was nearby, and on Saturdays, there would be a bus to take girls to the base for dances. A few girls in the sorority met their husbands that way. There was even talk of the Army using our sorority house, but influential alumnae kicked up too much of a fuss. Everybody was committed to the effort, and I look back on that with thankfulness. What would have happened to England and Europe if Hitler had been able to do what he had in mind is unimaginable.

§

My group of friends graduating from Kansas State College in 1943

I graduated from college when I was twenty and got a job on the *Topeka State Journal*. I moved to Topeka, Kansas, where I shared a walk-up apartment with several friends, and worked on that daily newspaper. Part of my beat was downtown Topeka, where there were various local and state offices and courts. Included in that area was the Navy recruiting office. I became friends with the people there and began stopping by on my beat and, eventually, talking about the WAVE officer-training program at Smith College. I had always dreamed about going to Smith; it was part of another—Ivy League—world. In addition, the war effort was more and more consuming, and finding a way to get more involved seemed compelling. The Navy would not take my application, however, until I turned twenty-one, so I had to wait.

I went to Smith College to become a WAVE officer in 1943.

After my July birthday, I applied for Officer Training in the Navy WAVES at Smith College, and they accepted me. My training started in October, and I worked at the paper through September and then left. I took the train to North Hampton, Massachusetts. My parents were very supportive, the way they had always been (except when I had some crazy, dangerous scheme, as I did from time to time). The war was also so pervasive that they must have expected my eventual involvement. For months after I left Kansas, my mother sent me the comics, which I was addicted to then, a way of showing support. That was the beginning of our correspondence; Mother and I sent letters back and forth to each other for years.

I arrived in Northampton, Massachusetts, in October of 1943, and when I experienced that beautiful fall weather and saw the incredible landscape, I thought, *I'm not sure I'm ever going to live in Kansas again.* I have loved the Northeast ever since.

The training at Northampton had many aspects. Interesting women from all over the country were in the very tightly structured program. We had classes in Navy history and protocols. We marched, too, including down to Wiggins Tavern where we had all our meals. We lived in one of the beautiful dormitories that had originally been a home. Training lasted two months, and then we got our commissions and had a little leave.

After we finished the training at Northampton, a group of us went to New York City. That was my first New York visit, and although the details of the trip are hazy, the feeling of being in New York stayed with me. It was the real beginning of my adult life.

After the leave, I was assigned to communications school at Mount Holyoke. So I got to "attend" another "Sister" college, as I went to Mount Holyoke for two months of training. There I learned Morse code and all about encryption, coding, and decoding. Leaving Mount

Holyoke, I was both an officer and a communications spe-
cialist, and was assigned to Washington.

*In New York during WAVE training
with my cousin Eloise Ray and friend*

*With Lisa Kestler and Ursula Breher-Kossler, who were
my close friends in the WAVEs and for many years after*

When I first arrived in Washington, I lived near Du-Pont Circle in an old embassy that had been turned into a boarding house. There were some truly eccentric people who lived there, including a woman who ironed in the nude. My roommate was a friend from college who had a degree in architecture and was working for the Navy Department. I had some very adventurous friends then, and that time was fun, if frantic, due to our involvement with the war effort.

In the early years in Washington, we worked shifts around the clock: two days of seven-to-three, and we would be off, then two days of three-to-eleven, then we would be off for eighteen hours, and then work eleven to seven at night. We were working around the clock, coding, decoding messages and routing them to the proper places. For example, we might send submarine-situation locations out to ships at sea. It was exciting work, even though these were really technical or secretarial jobs. In the Navy at that time, every dispatch over the classification of "confidential" could only be handled by a commissioned officer. That was a huge part of our usefulness as officers—it freed up men, young ensigns, to go out to sea, while we were handling all the paperwork. Those years in Washington were very rewarding; we really felt part of what was happening in the world.

After a few months I moved out to Alexandria to live with my cousin Eloise Ray, who worked at the Pentagon. She had originally come to Washington with her husband, who was in the Army. When they got divorced, I moved in with her. We had known each other as children, of course, but Eloise was older, and we did not really have much in common. Eloise was very goal-oriented and fashion-conscious. She was far more sophisticated and worldly than I was, and was also very beautiful in the style of a *femme fatale*. While we lived together, however, even though we were so different in so many ways, we became friends. Then Eloise moved on to New York, and when the war ended, I decided to stay another year. I moved into the Broadmoor Hotel on Connecticut Avenue with three fun roommates, including one of my best friends from the Navy, Ursula Breher from North Dakota. She was charming and personable, and everybody adored her. It was a wonderful time. We all had off-and-on boyfriends, but nothing serious. We just soaked in that upbeat atmosphere that was everywhere in Washington in the months after the war.

On leave from the Navy, I met with Kansas State professor C. J. Medlin to receive an award for the yearbook I edited.

I was in the service for three years and got promoted to Lieutenant (j.g.). One of the reasons I stayed the extra year was that I had a good friend who had a job in the Bureau of Personnel as a congressional liaison. She pulled some strings and got me transferred there, and that was a blast. First of all, it had regular working hours instead of around-the-clock shifts, and second, we had that great apartment at the Broadmoor Hotel. We enjoyed our jobs; work often consisted of going to meet with congressmen in their offices and having lunch with them. We were not exactly making policy. The congressmen would have constituents whose sons had not been discharged properly or who were asking for help with another issue. We were there to take instructions from the congressmen about how we could be helpful, and then we would go draft letters and send them. It was fun; I learned a lot and stayed in for almost an extra year. Finally, I decided to go to graduate school on the G. I. Bill.

§

After the war, the G. I. Bill transformed this country in such a profound way. It allowed servicemen and women to come back and go to college. It created this whole new body of educated young people and an attitude of optimism throughout my generation. I decided it was a good pathway for me. I enrolled at the University of Minnesota, which had a wonderful journalism program. I was going to get a graduate degree, however, in political science, which I thought would be useful in my career as a journalist.

Having grown up in the Midwest, I knew Minnesota was a very good school. I also had a boyfriend I had met in Washington. He had been in the Army, but had gotten out the year before I did, and was going to the University of Chicago to finish law school. Going to Minnesota meant that we would be close enough to visit back and forth and stay in touch.

When I got out of the Navy, I went to New York for a final-fling visit with my cousin and several friends I had met in the Navy. My cousin Eloise was then the fashion editor of *Charm* magazine. She was having a successful career in New York, and she had just lucked into a walk-up apartment at 58th and Madison and was looking for a roommate. Of course, I did not think about her need for a roommate seriously because I was going to graduate school, but I did have a wonderful few days in New York with all these friends. Then I took the train out. My plan was to go to Chicago, visit my boyfriend there, and then go up to Minneapolis to confirm my enrollment in graduate school and my job as a dorm counselor, which would pay for my room and board. So, I said goodbye to my New York friends, took the train to Chicago, and had a couple of days there with my boyfriend. At the end of that visit, I realized that he was not going to be in my future.

He took me to the station to get the train to go to Minneapolis and confirm all my plans. That train was on one track. And on the opposite track was a train to Kansas City. I cannot even really explain what happened next.

I did not get on the train to Minneapolis. In what seems to me now such an impulsive decision, an intuitive leap of faith, perhaps, I got on the train to Kansas City instead, then on to Manhattan, Kansas. I was going home. Temporarily. I announced to my family that I was not going to school as planned after all. Instead, I was going to New York to seek my fortune.

The Career Track

I still to this day do not know what happened on that train platform, but I do know one thing about my decision: I have never regretted it for one single moment. I think Eloise lucking into that apartment was a big part of what happened. I could not resist the allure of that situation, especially not after I had given up on the relationship that had, in part, drawn me back to the Midwest.

Eloise would not get the apartment until December, however, and this was August, so I had to find something to do until the apartment was available. By some incredible coincidence, the editor of the daily paper in Manhattan, where I had worked as a young person, quit. As a temporary measure, the paper hired me as the new editor. They knew I was not going to stay, but it was an emergency, and I would fill in while they looked for the right person. So, within weeks of arriving home, I had a job as editor of the *Manhattan Mercury-Chronicle*.

I had a sports editor, a society editor, and an Associated Press editor working for me. I wrote a daily column and the editorials, did most of the editing, some reporting, and set the headlines. I was working eighteen hours a day, no question about that. It was probably as demanding as any job I have ever had. Anyway, it brought in a little income, and it kept me busy. I was getting the paper out every day, although the management did not really like my "socialist" editorials. So I think it was okay with everybody when I announced that I would be leaving.

Eloise got the apartment in December, and I left for New York. I think those years in the WAVES gave me confidence that I could find work. When I got to New York and moved into our 58th Street walkup, I very soon registered with a temp agency, and that is how I paid the rent and supported myself at first. Because of the Navy, I had terrific secretarial skills for that time—before computers, of course. I could type, take shorthand, and do clerical work. I was in high demand at the agency, so I worked all over New York. I learned the city that way. I worked at Rockefeller Center, Wall Street, uptown and downtown, and began to feel I could manage my life in the city. Then I put an ad in the *New York Times* because I wanted to do editorial research. (I did not think I had the qualifications to get a job writing for the *New York Times* just yet!) From my ad, I got a job working as an assistant and researcher for Freling Foster, a columnist for *Collier's Magazine*. He worked out of his apartment on East 70th Street, which was not far from where I lived, so I would walk there and back.

His process was unique. His weekly column was called "Keep Up with the World." Readers of the magazine were invited to submit leads for stories, anything from local news to interesting phenomena. It could be historic, athletic, or a current event—any event, anywhere in the world. If a reader's story was chosen, he or she would receive ten dollars. So Freling would pick a handful, about eight to ten, every week, to tie together in a column. It was a very innovative concept for a time before global media or the Internet. My job was researching the stories and validating the content. I would spend hours almost every day at the library. For me, going to the New York Public Library to research was a dream job. I had always loved the library as a child because it was a place where you could immerse yourself in learning. As an adult, I found this to be even more true, and so going to work every day was almost a privilege.

This was not just any library either. The New York Public Library had a scale and presence that was unmatched. Of course it was pre-digital, so you would go all over looking up things. While I was primarily researching, I also learned a lot of writing skills from Freling Foster. He taught me how to weed out what was relevant and interesting and make a story from it. I learned how to take a million different strands of a story and tie them together, how to boil facts down to their essence. After a while, though, I knew that however much I learned from Foster, in career terms, there was nowhere to go from there.

§

I was not actively looking for a job, but I found one anyway, through my dear friend from Kansas, Polly Hathaway. Growing up in Kansas, we met in junior high and became best friends at age eleven. We remained best friends for a couple of years before her family moved away from Kansas to Maryland. Polly came back for one year at Kansas State, then returned and graduated in Maryland. She married Neal Hathaway right out of college and was living in Washington when I moved there, so we reconnected. She and her husband then moved to New York, and we reconnected again in New York. A year or so after I was working for Freling Foster, Neal was working at CBS as head of program promotion. Through him, I got an interview at CBS, and they hired me to do program promotion. I loved the whole idea of it: working at 485 Madison and all the prestige and excitement that went along with it. It was also a wonderful time to do promotion for shows at CBS: we had Edward R. Murrow as our big star, as well as a lot of other major talent in the network. Television was just coming into its own—what a fun job!

As luck would have it, Polly's brother Jerry Hardy was also in New York, working for Doubleday. Through Jerry, I met a group of friends who had all attended the University of North Carolina at Chapel Hill, and we became a little crowd that did things together. We went to the theater, down to the village, and on nice weekends we would make the trip out to Jones Beach. A few of the guys were living in a walk-up apartment in a brownstone on East 59th, across from Bloomingdale's. That became our base. We all had interesting jobs—it seemed everybody was a journalist or a filmmaker. We were living the New York life, although not the expensive New York life by any means. It was not necessary then. So many activities were free, and it only cost about ten cents to ride the subway, although we often walked anyway because we loved to explore on foot.

§

Jerry had become friends with Michael Erlanger when they were in the Army together. Michael was now back in his hometown, New York City, an eligible young bachelor and at that time president of the BVD Corporation. This was a family business that his grandfather and great-uncle had started. Jerry was setting Michael up with every single girl he knew, and I made the list. So Jerry and his wife, Tommy, invited Michael and me to dinner, just the two of us, in their apartment in Peter Cooper Village. Michael and I connected that night. Michael was so different from me and from anybody I'd met in my life. To say it was love at first sight would not be exactly true. It was "like" at first sight, and connect at first sight, and comfortable at first sight. We started dating after that evening, in the fall of 1948.

We went out several times. Each date was enjoyable, even exhilarating, but I never thought those outings would add up to anything serious. I was not exactly needy when I met Michael. I knew who I was at that point, at least enough for then. I had a certain amount of self-confidence that came with having gone through the WAVES and come to New York. I had made a life in the city and

was having a reasonably successful career. I was not looking for a serious relationship, but it was a really interesting connection. We actually saw so many things the same
way. We both loved the theater and going gallery hopping.
Above all, we loved to laugh, and each of us knew from the
beginning how to make the other smile.

Politics was also a bond. Budding political activists, we
became involved in the young veterans' political groups
that were meeting in New York. Of course, the atmosphere
was still very post-war, and there was a special energy with
our young veterans. Michael had been in the Army for several years, the National Guard, then the Air Force, and,
ultimately, in Army intelligence. Along the way he met
Jerry Hardy and they became friends, a friendship which
so greatly influenced our lives.

§

I was at a New Year's Eve party that year (1948) with my
crowd and remember calling Michael and saying, "Well,
this is a good party. You really should come over." It was
New York. It was that kind of time. He came, and at this
party, we arranged to have brunch the next day, New
Year's Day. He picked me up at my apartment the following morning to go to brunch. I liked his family, and they
seemed to like me, and so after brunch we went to call on
his mother and wish her Happy New Year. The Erlangers
had a beautiful, elegant house on 64th between Park and

Lexington, and I loved going there. While we were sitting in the library, talking to Michael's mother, he said, "Mary and I are thinking of getting married." I almost fell off the sofa!

It was the first I had heard of this plan. I could not make a scene right there, so I just decided to go with it—we would talk about it later. His mother was thrilled, probably because she was anxious for him to get settled in the world. He was thirty-three, and I was twenty-six. We did talk about it later, of course, and we decided to go for it. I do not think he had really thought through what effect his announcement would have on me. He decided he wanted to marry me and believed in that plan with all his heart. The fact that I might not accept his proposal did not occur to him! That was just Michael. He was a true original. I have never met anybody like him; he was extremely intuitive. When he decided something, he was ready for it to happen.

Even contemplating us as a serious couple had been difficult for me because we came from such different backgrounds. I was from Kansas and the daughter of a minister. Michael's family was Jewish, if not practicing. At that point, Judaism had not played any role whatsoever in my life. I had known perhaps one Jewish girl in high school and knew virtually nothing about Jewish culture. I was worried our cultural backgrounds would come between us. While Michael himself never went to synagogue, his family very much identified as Jewish; they were part of the Jewish social set in New York and New Jersey. The richness of their lives—culture, art, music, and the involvement with the world—was so fascinating and wonderful to me. It still is. Perhaps I should not have worried. After all, I believe Michael's mother, "Kick," liked me because I was so different from the New York Jewish girls her son could have married.

I had had a fairly adventurous life so far, and Michael's mother was a rebel herself. Kick, or Alene Erlanger, was a very interesting woman. She spent a lot of her young life in Cuba, where her father was in partnership with her uncle in the tobacco business until they sold it and came back to New York. She went to Hunter College, as had her mother before her. She was beautiful and very talented, but influenced by a culture that did not encourage her to have an independent career. She was truly a woman ahead of her time. When I met Michael, I had been away from home for several years and was making my way in the world. I was different. I was a hick from Kansas, and she and Michael found that interesting. I had a wonderful relationship with her. She was a great role model, wonderful hostess, savvy, and fun. She loved a good time and really did love me. She was never cruel to me although she could be, at times, to others.

We had Kick's blessing from the moment Michael impulsively announced our engagement, but I had to write my parents a letter with the news. Michael had made quite an impression on me, of course, so they had some introduction to him through my letters. In hindsight, it was not, however, the introduction I would have given him. Michael had racehorses. This fact had greatly impressed me when I first met him. In November I was writing my parents letters about being in New York, and my adventures, and I wrote, "I met this man who just sent his racehorses to Florida for the winter." Now, it turned out that this man was going to be their son-in-law.

Michael and I went out to visit my parents, and they liked Michael and were very welcoming, and said they would come to New York for our wedding. At that point, we were planning a June wedding in the country. Patience, however, was not one of Michael's many virtues, and we changed the plans to New York City in March.

We cut the wedding cake for some fifty guests.

Michael and I were married in his parents' home in New York City.

So, on March 12, 1949, my father married us in Michael's family's home on East 64th Street in New York. Eloise was my maid of honor; Jerry was the best man. Although our wedding was very simple, about fifty people in total, Kick knew how to throw a good party; the event was elegant.

Much later, at our fiftieth anniversary party, Jerry's wife, Tommy, wrote a long letter to be read aloud, saying that at the dinner they invited Michael and me to, the occasion of our first meeting, she and Jerry might as well not have been there at all.

Mrs. Michael Erlanger

I t was a huge shift in identity. It was one thing to be Mary Margaret—or Mary Peg, my nickname—Arnold, the career girl in New York, and it was quite a different thing to be Mrs. Michael Erlanger. Being Mrs. Michael Erlanger added a whole other identity. I was the wife of a company president, and company presidents had their own world. In addition to having an important job with the family business, his whole history and family background were so drastically different from mine. There were those racehorses, for one thing. His whole world was just so different from mine that I had to find out where I stood: what parts of me fit and which parts I could adapt and still be authentically myself in this new life and environment.

Dinner at the Plaza Hotel, around 1950

I was reasonably good at my job at CBS, but it took tre-
mendous focus. I had always had a lot of energy, and I just
poured it into having a successful career. After we were married in 1949 (and a two-week honeymoon in Guatemala),
Michael still had a very demanding job, and I continued
to work at CBS. That work began to be harder and harder
for me after all these other responsibilities came into my
life. We had to be very involved with Michael's family and
friends. As time went on, it became harder to be the career girl. We were going to the theater, or somewhere else,
nearly every night. The pace of life was hectic. Finally, we
reached the point where we both needed a break of some
kind. We soon saw that travel could be our release. The
family company had textile connections abroad, especially
in Italy and Switzerland, and we jumped at the opportunity to visit Europe. So, in the spring of 1952, I quit my
job, he took a three-month leave from his, and we sailed to
Europe. We were on our own, rented cars, and tried to see
it all. I had never been to Europe; he had been only once,
and so we experienced it all together. We both loved travel,
and that was the first of many trips we would take over the
next fifty years.

§

In Venice on our first trip to Europe in 1952

When we returned to New York, we moved to a new apartment on East 70th Street: I really loved it. Within weeks, CBS asked me to come back to work to do network promotions, and I could not resist. I had made friends with a woman there, Carol Whedon, who was then running network promotion. I had the opportunity to work with her on network projects. When I first went to CBS, everyone worked for both radio and television. One day you would write promotion for a radio show and the next day for television. Then they divided, and I got assigned to television, an exciting prospect.

It was a great era for television. Working there was challenging because there was a lot of pressure at that level. I was writing press releases and speeches, often for the executives. I also wrote presentations for the Peabody

Awards and worked with the art department on ads for shows such as *Jack Benny* and *Ed Sullivan*. It was a much higher level than I had been at before. It was a very intense, almost-workaholic environment, even with the occasional midday martini.

I could not just go home at night and collapse, or even take work home to focus on it, because Michael and I had so many social obligations. We were also trying to have children. I finally reached a point where I knew that I needed to leave. It was impossible to do a really good job in that high-pressure situation. I knew I needed to take control and leave while I could be in charge. I had quit once before, of course, to take our trip, and so I had some confidence about what I needed to do and when to do it. Everything fell into place.

§

It began with house hunting. Michael's family had a weekend place in Elberon, New Jersey—on the Jersey shore, close to the beach. They had a stable there, his grandparents had a house, and his parents had another house. After the grandparents died, his parents remade this really beautiful, old house into a lovely weekend place. We had a little apartment down there, and they liked having us. We went out on weekends for a few years, but it was hardly an easy journey before the New Jersey and Garden State Parkways. Most importantly, the life there was not *our* life, the life we were interested in making for ourselves. So we had been looking at weekend places up in Connecticut where we had some friends.

Then, in 1954, Michael's grandmother died and left us ten thousand dollars. We decided to use that as a down payment for a house we had found in Ridgefield, Connecticut. We were supposed to confirm the offer the next weekend when Michael woke up one morning and said, "Oh, instead of using that money to buy that house, why don't we just go to Africa?" I said, "Okay." Just that simple. The trip to Africa had started as a vague dream, a "that's where we'd like to go next" idea. That decision was a perfect illustration of how impulsive Michael could be. So he took another leave from his job, I quit mine, and we went to Cook's Tours, and I said, "My husband and I want to go to Africa. Can you help us plan a two-month trip?" And they did.

§

Going to Africa on our own was adventurous—after all, it was 1954! We traveled first to Greece, then from Athens to Johannesburg—the only time in my life that I have seen and slept in a berth on an airplane! Johannesburg was totally in the throes of apartheid then; we were even warned not to walk outside our hotel at night. A highlight was being taken to the Saturday afternoon gathering in a small stadium, where groups of dancers from various tribes—all working in the diamond mines—performed. We took movies, and for years showed them to friends and interested groups.

In Africa in 1954

We had a guided tour of Kruger Park, our first of many views of lions, elephants, tigers, antelopes, and other amazing sights. Our guide protected us at night as we slept in a tent.

From Johannesburg we flew up the spine of Africa, all still under colonial rule—Southern Rhodesia and Northern Rhodesia, where Victoria Falls was the highlight—then flew to a tiny airport in what was then Ruanda-Urundi (now Rwanda). We were met by a guide from Uganda in his ancient sedan. We spent days with him, driving through the Congo, filled with unbelievable sights of the villages and wildlife, even a pygmy village. At one village, we were greeted like royalty, seated in chairs while the villagers performed their ritual dances just for us. (More movies, of course!)

Colonial rule and segregation prevailed, of course, and more than once we had to take food from a hotel (or hostel) dining room to our native driver, because they would not serve him.

Our final destination was Uganda, which had a much more progressive culture and integrated university and government. It was fascinating to see the elegantly robed natives gathering for meetings and banquets at our hotel in Kampala, the capital. Our driver had a small farm in the suburbs and took us to see it—we thought of him so many times in the years that followed, when disaster and tyranny enveloped Uganda.

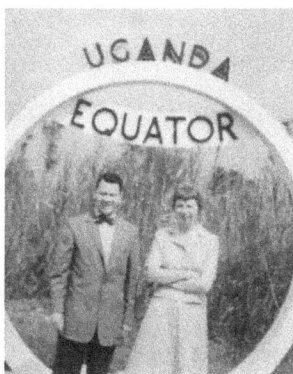

At the equator, 1954

Our original plan was to go from Uganda to Kenya, but when we went to the consulate for guidance, they advised us to skip it. The Mau Mau were active and making it dangerous for tourists in Kenya, so we decided to fly from Uganda to Capri, where we had some friends. It was beautiful and a wonderful place to wind down from our exciting trip.

The years that followed saw the end of colonialism, of course, and the rise of power struggles and violence that have enveloped Africa ever since. We treasured our incredible memories and followed the African developments with great interest and considerable heartache. We continued to get requests to show our African movies for years.

§

After we returned, Michael had to get back to work. The family company was changing a lot during those years. BVD (originally Bradley, Vorhees and Day) was an underwear business, which his grandfather and great uncle had started. It was a true innovation: instead of having the two-piece long-john style underwear, they came up with the ingenious idea of a single lightweight garment with short arms and legs. They were tremendously popular in their day; everyone had to have BVDs. So Michael's father and uncle developed textile mills in North Carolina to supply the factories.

We visited North Carolina regularly and were treated like royalty there. In the mill village, named Erlanger after the family, there was even a little section called Michael. Erlanger Day was celebrated once a year with a big, Southern-style barbecue. When I went there as the young bride, I met a wonderful family, the Robertsons. Julian Robertson was the CEO of Erlanger Mills. While her husband ran the mill, Blanche was a gracious person and a really wonderful role model for me. She made me believe that I could take on this role of being wife to the company president.

By the fifties, however, BVD was struggling because the factories in Baltimore were heavily unionized, and there was terrific competition from overseas. The underwear manufacturing part was suffering, although the textile business was thriving at that time. By the mid-fifties, BVD had been sold, and the textile business was the whole focus. As the years went on, and foreign competition increased, eventually the company struggled as textile manufacturing began to move to foreign shores. The company was gradually sold, so by the time Michael's father died in 1969, it had become more or less a family holding company with textile interests. Michael's mother also died in 1969 after a battle with cancer. Over the years Michael's responsibilities grew less and less as a result. I had quit my job in 1954, meanwhile, and I knew I was not going back to work any time soon. Our lives began to take a different direction.

Our Own Family

Michael and I had always wanted a life of our own and our own family. Our first major move was to buy a 1912 Dutch colonial house in East Chatham. New York, on the New York side of the Berkshires. We loved our weekends there and had streams of guests from the city; we all enjoyed the beauty of the area and all the entertainment: Tanglewood, Jacob's Pillow, and Music Barn—a venue owned by friends where we first heard Dave Brubeck and other stars of the era.

We also renewed our focus on having children—dealing with some fertility problems. We adopted a beautiful baby, Amy, five weeks old, in 1956. We got the call in East Chatham and drove into the city to begin our family life at our East 70th Street apartment. Of course, it was a life-transforming event.

Neither Michael nor I were well equipped to handle all the responsibilities of parenthood, and we were lucky to hire an experienced West Indian nanny, Dora Moses, who came a few days a week. She became a wonderful part of our lives, and stayed with us when our son, David, was born in 1959.

After that happened, we found that we needed a larger apartment, and also that the East Chatham weekend commute was too far and too difficult. We moved to a large duplex apartment on East 68th Street, and before too long decided to put our upstate New York house on the market.

We did not want to give up our weekend getaways. We began looking in northern Fairfield County—it was beautiful, and we had friends there. Then one day we went to a New York cocktail party for a friend who had moved his family to London when he took a two-year contract with the BBC. Will Roland was back for a brief visit, and needed a ride to Redding, Connecticut. We readily offered him a ride, as we had some dates with realtors in the area. It turned out that his temporary Redding renters were moving, and he had to see about his house. We drove him out, left him in Redding, and saw a series of Westport houses which did not appeal to us. We picked him up late that Saturday afternoon, and on the way back to the city, we arranged to "housesit" for the Rolands until we found our own house—and until they knew when they were returning from London. What a life-changing decision!

§

We realized we had lucked into the most beautiful town in Connecticut—and we fell in love with the 1810 house. Two years later, when our friends settled in London with a long-term contract, we bought "Lilac Hill Farm."

The house was beautiful, had wonderful energy, and was on a great piece of property—the only catch was that it needed everything done to it! It had not been touched in

We bought "Lilac Hill Farm" in Redding, Connecticut, in 1962.

Our first child, Amy, was born in 1956.

Our son, David, was born in 1959.

years, as far as repairs and updating. It seemed so demanding that we decided to sublet our New York apartment—
use the rental money to fix up our house—and I would stay
in Redding with the children to supervise the work. Michael would commute. Amy was just starting kindergarten, and David was about two and a half, so we concluded
that a year out of the city would not really be harmful to
them.

At the end of the year, I was the only one who wanted
to go back to New York. Michael loved the long commute
from Redding because he could read a book a day. And
the kids really loved being out there. We had also begun to
make friends with people who had young children, and a
new life was emerging. We decided to sell our apartment
and move full-time to Redding.

A Thanksgiving dinner with family and friends at our Redding home

After Michael's parents died in 1969, the house became the gathering place for his sisters and their children, plus our friends. Thanksgiving and Christmas were always celebrated there. Both Amy and David went to the Redding public schools—which were excellent for their time—then Amy finished high school at Andover and David at Exeter. Amy graduated from Georgetown and David from Julliard. Then came wonderful additions to our family. Amy married Randall Folkman in 1982, and had two daughters, Katie and Caroline, both raised in Redding. David married Jean Witter in 1993 and they had Aaron, still growing up in New York City, but coming to Redding on weekends. All have been a source of continuous delight.

Amy's wedding at our home in Redding

Our Connecticut Life

After we moved to Connecticut, I got involved in the schools, the PTA, and the League of Women Voters. Redding was a jewel: the town had some very good leadership early on with respect to zoning and was ripe for open-space acquisition. The state of Connecticut had a pioneer program for matching town funds for open-space purchases. Michael and I got very involved in that kind of advocacy and, ultimately, in the town politics. Our house became a gathering place; we got to know lots of wonderful people and made many, many friends in town. One of the best friends was Mary Anne Guitar, who became an environmental leader and served as first selectman for twelve years. Through the political experiences with our friends, I learned this: one of the most fulfilling things in life is to work for a cause you believe in with people that you like, respect, trust, and have fun with. There's just nothing that's more satisfying. Those years were very rich.

§

In our household, meanwhile, a country lifestyle meant that one thing was certain: animals. Michael had grown up between an aviary, a stable, and a kennel. His mother raised, bred, showed, and judged poodles, and she was head of the Canine Corps during World War II. When Michael

Redding life, around 1965

Our family in 1969

My father, Rev. J. David Arnold

Amy, David, Michael, and me, around 1980

In the mid-1970s, Amy and my friend Bea Shilstone had my friends make quilt squares and put them together in a spectacular quilt.

and I first married, we did not have any pets, but that was short-lived. In fact, the first Christmas we were married, Michael's mother gave us a dog. We then had to move because we needed a yard. From that time on, we always had dogs. Poodles were my favorite breed, and that is what we usually had, but after we moved to Connecticut, we had a real variety, including a Newfoundland and Australian terriers, which are wonderful little dogs.

Michael continued to be involved with horseracing, too. His mother actually bought his stable, but when she died he was back in the horse business. Horses were important to him, and he was very good with them. He would recite all the horse bloodlines when we went to yearling sales. It was always a strange world to me, but fascinating. When a window like that opens in your life, you can see a whole world you did not know anything about.

Inevitably, our life in Connecticut included saddle horses. Amy and Michael shared the passion for riding. In 1969 we took the children to Europe, and in Ireland we bought a horse for Amy, who did competitive riding through her high school years. Michael was very involved as head of the local Pony Club for several years.

David was the musician. He started with the piano and then the recorder, then the flute, then the bass. He was always into music, and stayed connected to it.

Of course, as time passed, my life changed. The children leaving marked the end of an era, and I began to spend more time in state-level activities: president of the state League of Women Voters, then government committees and the women's movement.

I learned a lot from the women's movement. I got to know many likeminded women, a lot of whom, like myself, had left careers to raise children. It was one or the other, career or family. There were also a lot of ways that women were discouraged from pursuing careers in the first place. I had been sheltered because I grew up in a college town, and was one of the "privileged" (although I did not know it at the time). Most of the young women I grew up with were expected to go to college, and somehow we all found a way to do that. Through the women's movement, I met many women in Connecticut from working-class families, who had to quit high school to go to work to put their brothers through college instead of going themselves! I learned a lot about the unfair ways women were treated and valued. It was an education for me.

§

I began to realize that I did have some exceptional role models within my own family. My mother managed to begin as a volunteer and transition to a salaried role as director of student programs in our church. Mother also had a cousin, Mary Margaret McBride, who was an inspiration to me, especially given that my name was also Mary Margaret. She was reared in Missouri, and as a young girl went to New York, where she had her own radio program, a daily show during which she interviewed publishers and authors and celebrities. She was a pioneer; quite a bit has been written about her. To me, she became an idealized role model. I remember thinking, "Here is a woman who has gone out on her own and made it in the world."

Looking back, the whole gender issue is far more complex than we saw it in the seventies, but the feminist movement was so powerful and had such good leadership. I was a delegate to the International Women's Year Convention in 1977—a huge gathering in Dallas that I will never forget.

In Connecticut, we knew that we wanted to pass an equal rights amendment. That was an impeccable cause, and we could really unite behind it. The same went for equal pay, career expectations, and household roles. Being in Connecticut put me in the middle of this struggle in a way that I never had been in New York City.

Birthdays and Family Legacies

While the cultural opportunities of the city were never too far away, we also looked for ways to bring that excitement out to us. Michael loved movies, and he had his favorites: *Seven Brides for Seven Brothers* (1952) was at the very top. It had wonderful dancers and singers, many of whom had impressive careers before and after. After we moved to Connecticut, I decided to rent *Seven Brides* for Michael's birthday celebration. This was back before DVDs, when renting a movie was much more involved. I had to send away for it and rent the projector and screen. We had a party and showed *Seven Brides for Seven Brothers* in the barn because it provided the best seating. The first party was a success, and so it became a tradition. For years on Michael's birthday, we rented that same movie and threw a party.

As the years passed, birthdays took on a different significance. In 1972, three of my close friends were turning fifty as well. Fifty sounded like the end of the world. *How would we ever get through this?* So, we decided we would get through by having a round of constant parties. We had them, our friends had them, and it was quite an unforgettable year, winding up with a house party on Block Island. By that time, we had a summer house on Block Island, which we bought when the children were teenagers. Our friends often visited with children. It was a wonderful house for that age and stage of life, where their friends and our friends could all stay at the same time. Block Island was a fitting place for the culmination party. Ever since then, for major birthdays, we four friends have thrown a party to celebrate—it has now gone on for forty years!

In the 1970s we bought an 1890s house on Block Island and spent many summer weeks there.

I am with visiting friends Polly Hathaway, Virginia Trotter, and Dorothy Higgins.

Bea and Arthur Shilstone are with us on Block Island.

I am with friends Bea Shilstone and Averill Loh on Block Island.

A house party on Block Island concluded a year of celebrating several 50th birthdays.

While we lived in Connecticut, I went back to Kansas to visit my parents regularly as long as they were alive. My father died when he was almost eighty, and I think he was very happy with his life. He seemed to have a true sense of being at peace with the world. My mother had that peace, too, but not to the same extent. I think having a special-

needs child really shaped her life, which she had to orga-
nize around that responsibility.

For the first year or two after my father died, she lived
alone with Louise in her house. Then she fell, and Louise had to call for help, which made Mother realize they
needed to be in a safer place. The two of them moved to
a retirement community in Topeka, Kansas. They moved
into adjoining apartments. Mother was seventy-five, and
she lived there for twenty-four years. After a few years, my
sister, Louise, developed Parkinson's, and she moved to
the nursing wing where Mother could still visit her often.
When I visited, I could spend time alone with Louise, who
had almost always been with Mother growing up. We truly
connected during those visits before Louise died in 1983,
and that connection was an unexpected gift.

At my mother's ninetieth birthday celebration

Around the same time, Mother began to lose her vision due to macular degeneration. She continued with most of her activities despite this problem; she taught Sunday school until she was eighty-seven years old. Even though reading was impossible for her, she never went completely blind. It was a relief that she was in a place with people who were very kind to her and loved her. She had a good support system.

Mother then got some of her vision back when a creative young eye doctor said, "Oh, you have cataracts. I'll take your cataracts off." When Mother had the surgery and regained some of her eyesight, she was already in her nineties, but the surgery improved her quality of life tremendously. Years before, she had taken charge of her exercise by walking, and after she could see, she could take her walks again. She could see her food again, and could do some reading and writing.

Mother lived to be ninety-nine and was a person of substance and interest, always. She was the pragmatist, while father was the people person. I am grateful that I inherited a little of both those traits. Both of my parents were authentic and compassionate, even in their old age. This greatly impressed me, but little did I know that my parents' aging would affect my career.

The Hartford Years

Politically, I had moved on to Hartford, the state capital. I was president of the state League of Women Voters for a couple of years. After I left that office, Ella Grasso, who was then governor, appointed me to several state boards and commissions. It was the time of the women's movement. I was very active in that, so I was appointed to the Commission on the Status of Women, and I was on a blue-ribbon committee that investigated the nursing home industry in Connecticut. I headed the subcommittee on Alternatives to Institutional Care, which was educational for me. I learned much about bureaucracy, but also about aging, and about people's needs. I really enjoyed the learning process and the feeling that I could bring about positive change. It was a successful project because we developed a package of legislation that created the ombudsman program in Connecticut, an advocacy program, and regulations for nursing homes designed to eliminate conflicts of interest—pioneer legislation for the early seventies.

Legislators were trying to reorganize state government at the time, and they did do a lot of reorganization, trying to simplify and stratify. They could not get anything through the legislature that reorganized human services, however, because there were too many turf issues. So the governor formed a blue-ribbon committee to do that and asked me to be the chair. I was very reluctant because I knew it was going to be really hard work, but somebody finally talked me into it. It was a challenge, but somehow they got hold of a little money for an office and some staff.

In the 1970s I worked closely with Connecticut governor Ella Grasso. This photo is from a League of Women Voters dinner honoring her.

For the next couple of years, we held hearings all over the state about human services, unmet needs, and conflicts of interest. At the end, we came up with a package of legislation based on those hearings. I don't even know what happened to that legislation because, again, the turf issues arose, and most of the proposals are still gathering dust in the capital archives. I learned a lot from that experience. It was worthwhile, but it was also very frustrating. One of the things I learned for myself about the political system was that—in some ways—the more power you have, the less you have. If you have carved out goals for yourself and you really want to get them accomplished, you have to wheel and deal and bend your own principles. I was not really good at that. When the panel came to an end, I realized I did not want to spend the rest of my life in politics. After all the years I was involved with the state in leadership roles, I had reached the end of my line and wanted to do something more one-on-one.

Meanwhile, Michael retired at the end of the sixties and built a really wonderful studio out of a little cottage that was attached to our barn, and he began writing a lot. He had two novels published while he was head of BVD. *Silence in Heaven* was published by Atheneum, and *Mindy Lindy May Surprise* by Random House. In Connecticut, he was able to immerse himself in writing, painting, sculpting, and all the creative things that he enjoyed. I was happy to see Michael enjoying his retirement, but I knew I was not ready for that yet.

§

My mother came from a long line of longevity genes; she lived to be ninety-nine. Her father lived to be ninety-seven. Her sisters also lived a long time. With all those genes, I figured I might have a few years ahead of me, and I decided to go back to school. As a girl, I would often accompany my father when he went out visiting old people. At the time that I decided to get out of the political world, I was visiting Mother regularly in the nursing home and realized I had a longstanding interest in gerontology. In my state job, I had learned quite a bit about aging and the needs of that population, and I was getting older myself. Because I wanted to work more one-on-one, instead of in the public arena, I decided to get a master's degree in counseling and specialize in gerontology. I was considering programs in Connecticut and New York. Then one day, I was in a phone conversation with Virginia Trotter, and a new plan began to take shape.

The Georgia Connection

Virginia Trotter was a childhood friend. She had grown up down the street from me, so I had known her for most of my life. We were like cousins; we were connected in so many ways. She had married right out of college, her husband was killed in the war, and she had gone back to graduate school and had a very distinguished career in academia. She was U. S. Secretary of Education under Presidents Nixon and Ford, then came to the University of Georgia as Vice President for Academic Affairs. When I told Virginia over the phone that I was thinking of going back to school, she said, "Oh, well, if you're going to do that, you need to come to Georgia. We have such good programs here." I said to Michael, almost as a joke, "Virginia says if I'm going to school, I should come to Georgia." There was a silence and then he said, "That's not a bad idea."

He was already retired. He had wanted to get out of the Connecticut winters for ages. He had had two heart attacks already, and was just open to a change of climate and scenery. We decided to go down and look it over.

I was fifty-eight, an unusual age at that time for women, or even men, to go back to school. Virginia rolled the red carpet out on that visit, however. She sent me to the right places and made it possible for me to see people who encouraged me to pursue my academic plans. We decided to go for a year and a half, kind of like a sabbatical from our real life. I would get a master's degree in counseling and the interdisciplinary gerontology certificate the University offered.

We could leave the house in Connecticut because we had a full-time caretaker, Allen Collier, a wonderful man who was with us for years and years. We knew he would look after the property. Amy was also living at home at that point. She had graduated from Georgetown (cum laude!) and was working on her MBA at a University of Connecticut program. Between them, they could look after the dogs and the house. We decided to go to Georgia; I was supposed to start in the fall of 1980, and we rented a house beginning in September of '80.

In June of 1980, however, Michael went for a heart check-up, and they took him by ambulance to Yale–New Haven Hospital—for a quadruple heart bypass. After the operation, doctors came out and told us it had been successful. At that point Amy had to leave, but David and I went to have lunch in the cafeteria. We heard them paging the doctors, and we came back. On the way to the recovery room after surgery, Michael's heart had stopped. They had to restart it several times with electricity, and he was in a coma for about a week after that. We did not know whether he would live or die or ever be himself again.

It was a near-death experience for him. Ultimately, Michael did pull through. He recovered consciousness and went home, but it was a long recovery. There was so much trauma. He said he even had to learn to brush his teeth again. The earlier heart attack had been very scary, of course, but there was no comparison. After the early attack we had gone along with the recommendations, and doing so seemed to work: Michael did not commute as often, and he recovered. Life went on. Then he had this bypass and actually died. Everything shifted. It cemented our relationship, if it needed any cementing: I knew so deeply that I did not want to lose him.

§

After Michael's crisis, we were not sure what to do about our plans to move to Georgia. We had rented a house in Athens and made plans. We postponed my enrollment at Georgia until January, but we went down in November to stay two or three weeks and see what the house we had rented was like. During our visit, people were very welcoming, and once again we had a great time. So we returned home just for Christmas and then moved to Georgia, and I started school in January of 1981. Michael and I lucked into Athens, just the way that we had lucked into Redding years before. This connection, too, turned out to be wonderful.

§

There was no comparison between the climates, and I loved being back in school. This move was really great for both of us. Michael liked Athens very much, too—it was liberating for him, actually. He had grown up in a family with many expectations and protocols. He really embraced our new life. It was a different culture, but people liked him and us for being different. They truly enjoyed Michael for who he was. He enjoyed his new life so much and lived in a community of creativity. He was in a men's group that meant so much to him—I think he was a mentor for many of them, and that bond meant the world to him. He also did a lot of drawing and painting, and he self-published eight volumes of poetry besides a book of short stories, and a play, which they put on at the Cellar Theatre one year. We also started doing a lot of New Age things together, such as dream work. We connected with the Unitarian church, which we had joined in New York City in 1954. Then the Unitarian minister, Terre Balof, became a close friend to both of us.

Michael's play S.A.M.I. *was produced at the University of Georgia in 1984.*

Michael was appointed to the board of the Georgia Museum of Art soon after we got to Georgia. Bill Eiland, the director, became a close friend. We both got really involved with the museum; doing so was a continuation of our passion for art, as we had started collecting in the early years of our marriage. We were married for seven years before we had children, and at that time we were living in the city. On weekends we would go from one art gallery to another, seeing what interested us. Michael had a wonderful eye; he was very intuitive. He could walk into a room and spot the best painting immediately. It was fun; our tastes were similar to begin with and kept forming as we went to galleries and museums. This was in the 1950s when there was some interesting stuff going on, for example abstract expressionism, and there were various artists we got interested in. We did not collect Andy Warhol, unfortunately, but we did collect pieces that we loved and began to assemble a collection of art that had meaning for us.

Some years later, after we moved from New York to Connecticut, we began to collect what are called animalier, small bronze sculptures created in the last half of the nineteenth century and the first part of the twentieth century. They were pieces that were fun to look for in New York and London and Europe and the various places we traveled. In the end we assembled quite a good collection of animaliers, which we gave to the Georgia Museum in 1996. They have quite a few pieces on display now in the museum, and the collection travels a lot, too. We have given them some paintings as well, including one of my favorites, *Beatnik Girl* by Jack Levine.

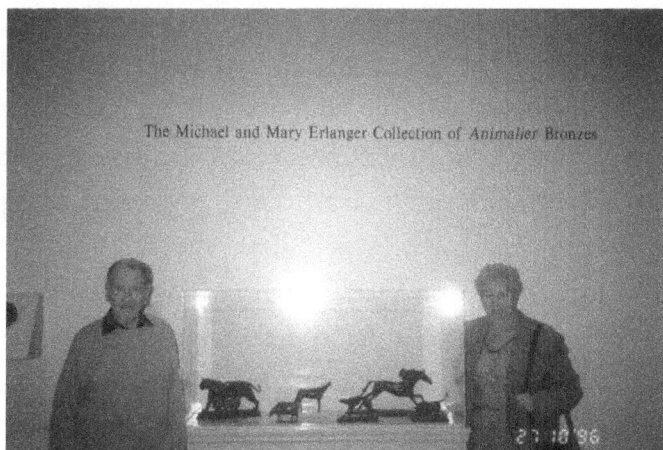

Michael and I donated our collection of Animalier bronze sculptures to the Georgia Museum of Art in 1996.

When we came to Georgia, we also got interested in folk art because while there was not the same gallery scene, there were some really interesting folk art and folk art-ists. We visited museums and galleries in the Georgia and North Carolina mountains and in Athens, too. The pieces were very different from the things we had collected in our New York era, and it was fun to find them together.

§

In Athens, we had started in a furnished house. We did not really like being in anybody else's space at all. We al-

ways liked doing things to our house. We were nesters, I
guess. When our lease was up, a friend of ours who was
in real estate suggested we look at Drayton Square, a new
well-built and interesting development. We thought it
looked like a good investment and a good place to live.
So, we were among the first to move into Drayton Square.
We had some furniture in storage from our New York
apartment; we shipped it down and had fun setting up
housekeeping.

We figured, "We're here for who knows how long it'll
take me to do this program, and then we'll just sell it and
go back to Connecticut." We, of course, had held on to our
house up there. So, we started to really live in Georgia and
loved being in Drayton Square. In fact, we sold our first
place and moved to a unit that was a little bigger in a few
years, about the time I finished my doctorate, in 1987. We
had always thought that when I finished we would go back
to Connecticut. Somehow, that just did not happen.

All the time I was in school in Georgia, we always
went back to Connecticut for the summers and thought
of that as our home. When I went into practice, however,
things changed. Originally, I was just going to get a master's degree in counseling and the gerontology certificate.
I saved up all my internship hours to do back up north at
the Danbury Hospital, where I had my connections and
assumed that if I ever worked or did anything with this
new training, it would be up there. We went along with the
plan, but by the time I went up for that training, I knew

I wanted much more education. I knew if I was going to do any kind of work with this, that I just wanted so much more knowledge and training. I did the nine months up in Connecticut. Amy got married while we were up there, and it was fun to be back with everybody, but we decided to return to Georgia to continue my education. I applied for the doctoral program and was accepted. In January of 1983, I started the doctoral program. I loved being in school once again.

We truly enjoyed life in Georgia; there was music, theater, dance, art, and good food and good company. Jack and Jane Payne were often companions, especially for the annual Spoleto Festival in Charleston, where we saw the best of everything. Our life became so manageable and exciting. If I had gone back to Connecticut and gone into practice, the logistics of life and a harsher climate would have really slowed us down. We both really enjoyed the diversity and stimulation. We both had lives of our own, but we also had a lot of interests that we pursued together.

Ultimately, I am confident that Michael lived years longer in Athens than he would have if we'd stayed up north. In part, that is because of the climate, but also just because of the manageable aspects of life. We had been holding on to our Connecticut house, which we loved, but as time went on, we realized it was impractical. We were not planning to return, our caretaker was getting old, and an 1810 house requires constant maintenance. We finally decided it was time to sell and settle in Athens permanently. We sold our Drayton Square abode and bought a house in Princeton Mill. Then we went up north and sold the house in Connecticut and distributed a lot of possessions.

We were committing to our new life, with one small exception. Years before, we had bought a second house in Redding because it adjoined our property. You could not see either house from the other, and the style was completely different. This was a modern "deckhouse." It was more like a vacation house you would find in Vermont or New Hampshire. We had rented it for years; the bottom floor was my son-in-law's lithography studio, and the top floor was an apartment. When we sold our home in Redding, we told our tenants that they had to leave; we did some renovations and kept it as a summer place and somewhere to celebrate holidays.

§

It was surely the best decision I ever made: to go back to school and move to Georgia. It was an extremely stimulating, productive time. For one thing, I was beginning a new career. I decided to work in marriage-and-family therapy, which became my passion. As UGA did not offer a doctorate in marriage and family then, I was technically getting my doctorate in counseling, but I took all my electives in marriage and family. Then there was a wonderful professor, Karen Wampler, who had come to establish an interdisciplinary certificate program in marriage-and-family therapy and the doctorate pathway: both exist to this day. We became very good friends, and she was an excellent mentor. I was in the first group to get that certificate.

I did many hours of practica at the Athens Family Counseling Center, then headed by Don Randall, who was also in the doctoral program with me. He had a seminary degree, a master's in counseling, and lots of special training in marriage-and-family therapy. I had been in a doctoral class that he was teaching at the university, so I knew him very well professionally. He left his job at Family Counseling and took a suite of offices at the Butler Building to go into private practice with Tom Camp, a pastoral counselor at the hospital. They needed another person for the space, and I needed hours for licensure. I decided to join them.

Don Randall and I started Athens Associates for Counseling and Psychotherapy in 1987. The group in the photo were with us for about twelve years: (from left to right) Ed Risler, me, Robyn McDonald, Mary Zorn Bates, and Don Randall.

Within a couple of years, I had decided to stay, and Don and I started Athens Associates for Counseling and Psychotherapy. Tom started the Samaritan Counseling Center, and in a couple of years we moved to better space at 598 South Milledge. As Samaritan grew, it moved to another space, but we stayed. There were five of us who were in practice together there for about twelve years: Ed Risler, Mary Zorn Bates, Robyn McDonald, Don, and me. Those were wonderful years. I stayed on in Athens much longer than I had planned when deciding to go back to school. At the beginning, I did not even know I would be doing that kind of work, necessarily, or that I would be able to have a successful career in the field. As it turns out, I had a wide range of clients of all ages and did a lot of supervision and guest teaching for the marriage and family program at the university. My specialty, however, was always aging, and I did a lot of training and speaking at workshops in those early years, which helped me carve out a niche. For years, I was the only person in Athens who was really specializing in working with older adults and families.

My career in counseling was an incredible gift to myself. I would say this for several reasons. First, it's a gift to feel that you are really able to help someone who is in a difficult time in his or her life. I am not talking about a really serious mental illness—people who come for therapy are usually in times of transition. They need a safe place to process what's going on, and that is what a good therapist provides. It is very satisfying to be able to provide that environment and feel that it has been helpful to someone who is struggling with the stress of a transition. Second, I never worked with anybody without learning something about myself. Therapy is an incredible way to really *be* there for somebody, and so you also explore the parts of yourself that need to be peeled away and looked at. Furthermore, the training and multitude of professional workshops beyond doing therapy continually develop intuition and ways to get to know yourself in depth. Just learning to accept yourself the way you are, and understanding what's about you and what's about somebody else is absolutely crucial to being authentic and being at peace with yourself.

I got my doctorate in 1987 (pictured with my granddaughter Katie, who was not quite two).

At a UGA football game with friends, around 2008

A plane-load of friends from Redding, Connecticut, joined us in Athens to help celebrate our fiftieth wedding anniversary.

Dancing with Michael at our fiftieth anniversary

Virginia Trotter helps celebrate Michael's eightieth birthday.

Katie came to UGA in 2004 as a Foundation Fellow. Here we are shortly before her graduation.

Adventures and Losing Michael

Every year we took a trip, somewhere. We really have been many, many places in the world. Since our first trip, we have been to Europe many times. We took the children to South America, to Japan, the Caribbean, and various other places. We went to Vienna and Russia with David. Alone, Michael and I went to China early on, and we went to India, Nepal, and Burma the winter before Michael had that first heart bypass. I have thought of that so many times since because if he had gotten sick at any point on that trip, there was not one place where we could have trusted the medical attention, if, indeed, we could have gotten any. But that was a fabulous trip. I have recently been reading about Burma (Myanmar) and so on and the sites that we saw there. It was really untouched by western culture at that time. They would allow tourists in for a little window of time, and then they'd shut it down again.

When we took a trip, it would trigger a thought of where we might want to go next. I remember that we went to Greece with a couple who were friends of ours, who had been on some trip where they found a wonderful guide who did private guiding. So we all decided we would go to Greece and hire this woman. It was a great trip, and we fell in love with Crete and its history of Egyptian connections. The guide said, "You know, if you like Crete, you must go to Egypt next." Well, okay. And then she said, "If you are going to Egypt, you must go with Swan's Tours because it's an English company, and they've been taking people to Egypt for years and years, and it'll be so much better then any other way you could go." We had never taken a tour before. We had always traveled totally on our own, but we thought we would take her advice, and so we went on this tour. That trip is still one of the most incredible trips of my life.

We were on a small ship—probably fifty people, for at that time only small boats could go the whole length of the Nile. (That changed when they opened up some of the locks.) It was so hot that we had to leave the boat by 6:00 a.m. to be back on board by noon so we wouldn't die of the heat. Everybody got sick from the water. It was a nightmare in many ways, but it was a fabulous trip, too. Again, that was the first tour we went on, and it opened us up to the possibility of guided tours. We were not enthralled by the big 3,000 passenger events, but we did go on to take a number of smaller tours. We took some more Swan's Tours and Museum of Natural History tours with great guides. Tours are not as adventurous as traveling on your own, but tours have advantages, like a level of expertise and delicious food; it was truly the former that attracted us to them.

On many trips, including some of the Museum of Natural History tours, we traveled with our friends Joan and Pete Repetti. Pete had been Michael's New York at-torney, and we all shared an appetite for travel and adventure. Some of our traveling highlights included a wonderful trip through Indonesia and a train trip from Berlin to Istanbul. The first trip we took with Pete and Joan, however, was to Japan, and we took the children with us, too. We had a friend who married a Japanese woman, Toshiko Toland, and we planned our 1971 trip to coincide with her going back to visit her parents. We wanted her to be our guide part of the time. She gave us a very different view, one not available to many tourists at that time. On that trip, we learned to love Japanese food and from then on, whenever we'd go to New York, we'd go to a good Japanese restaurant.

China was also a great adventure. We went to China in 1979, which was very early. We had wanted to see China ever since Nixon went, and they had just opened up to ordinary "tourists," and opportunities were limited. So, when our travel agent called in January and said, "I have this trip leaving February 15th for China," we started packing right away. In China, they were still wearing the blue Mao uniforms, and there were very few Westerners, almost no cars, and certainly no modern hotels. It was fascinating. There were some places we went where people came out and lined up on the street to see us because they had never seen Westerners. A highlight of that trip was seeing, in Xian, part of the terracotta army, which was just being excavated. We really wanted to go back to China after all the changes, but never made it.

We took a three-month trip to Europe in 1952, sailing over on the Ile de France.

We visited Venice in 1952 . . .

and again in 1992 (on a trip with Marilyn and Jack Kehoe).

In Egypt in 1972

Drinking champagne in a hot-air balloon over France, 1987

Michael and I went to Italy several times. We took some trips with Marilyn and Jack Kehoe, founder and head of the UGA program in Cortona, who would lead students all around Italy and then, after we begged him to, a few trips with the older crowd. Those were wonderful trips.

In 1987, the year I got my Ph.D., I took the summer off, and we scheduled a trip to Paris and a barge trip on the river Seine. We almost did not go. A few days before we were supposed to leave, I got test results that suggested I had breast cancer. We decided to go ahead with the trip. We did not talk to anyone about the tests, but on one of our last days I learned incidentally that one of our traveling companions had undergone a mastectomy twenty-five years ago, which helped me gain some perspective. I had my mastectomy when we returned to Georgia, without any radiation, and was back to my family-counseling job soon after.

Michael did have another quadruple bypass in 1991. When he had his first one, in 1980, they told us that, although it was fairly new surgery at the time, research was showing it would last at least ten or eleven years. So in '91, Michael went to Emory to have another one. At Emory, the whole corridor was filled with men who had had a bypass ten or more years ago! He underwent the surgery and came through that very well; then later on, he had two hip replacements and a shoulder replacement—all at different times. He was a good healer and, indeed, he was a survivor; those substitutions worked for him until the end, and he never mentally declined.

Unfortunately, the last six months of his life were very hard for him due to his heart problems and a nerve injury in his shoulder from a pacemaker surgery. He was in pain and miserable; he was really ready to move on. There was nothing ahead for him but suffering and misery. So, on one visit to the doctor, Michael said, "I want you to send me home with Hospice." The doctor responded, "That's fine." Michael lived a very short time after that. He died on February 21, 2002.

§

We celebrated the fact that Michael did have such a long, wonderful life. We were also able to travel; every year we managed to get in a trip, and we were still traveling up until a year before he died. All those years we had were so treasured. Michael was a good role model in looking at his own reactions and working on them. Reading and re-reading his books, especially his late-life poems, I realized how valuable his observations were and how he used his transitions of health, particularly, to gain strength and insight into himself. What a remarkable man!

Coming Full Circle

It took me a long time to decide to move back to Connecticut after Michael died. I did not want to give up my practice, and I did not want to give up my Athens life. Having worked with older people all these years, however, I knew that when you get old, you really need to be near family. You need somebody who can take charge, and you need to make important decisions while you are still able, before you have them made for you. So the summer I turned eighty-six, I decided it was time for me to really make a plan. I started winding down my practice that fall and focused on selling my house.

There was no question about where I would live in Connecticut. By then, a very nice retirement community had been developed in Redding, Connecticut, the town where we had lived all those years. I decided it was time for me to move there. I had friends there, and Michael and I happened to have signed up for it years before when it was on the drawing board by putting down a small deposit. We were just never really ready to go, even as the facility gradually got built. It took a long time to build Meadow Ridge, but it's now a very nice place, with some 400 residents. Altogether, it is a campus with an independent-living section, a smaller assisted living unit, and a reasonable-size healthcare center where people can go if they get sick, after surgery, or if they need round-the-clock care. It's a safe place, very well run, with good activities, and there are lots of very good reasons to be there.

I moved to Meadow Ridge in Redding, Connecticut, in 2009.

I moved to Meadow Ridge in 2009. Having an unbelievable gift of hospitality from my dear friend Lynda Walters has made it possible for me to have a long Athens visit every winter since I moved up north. Not only do I escape the Connecticut snows, but I can reconnect with the rich life of Athens and many, many good friends and colleagues.

I live in a nice, comfortable apartment with a good bit of wall space. I have a lot of drawings and some paintings, art that we lived with for years. An interesting and diverse group of people live at Meadow Ridge. Most are from areas in New York or Connecticut, but people also come from all over the country because they have children in the area. Most move in with the same motivation I had, except, because I lived in Redding all those years, I have the advantage of knowing the community, and I know my way around. I did not have to learn the winding Redding roads. At this stage of my life, I cannot imagine having to do that! It was a good move, and I am where I need to be. My grandchildren Katie and Caroline and Aaron are all wonderful parts of my life, as are my children, Amy and David, and my daughter-in-law, Jean.

David and Jean with their son, Aaron, born in 2003

David and Jean on a visit to Georgia

We took the Folkman family to Alaska in 1996: Caroline, Amy, Randall, and Katie.

In 2012 I went to Costa Rica with Aaron, David, and Jean (not pictured).

Caroline on her twenty-first birthday with her sister, Katie

Polly Hathaway and I have been friends since we were eleven. We are still hanging out together at Meadow Ridge.

Family was a powerful motivation for me to return to Connecticut. My daughter lives in Redding, in a house that she and her husband built for their family. Their two daughters, Katie and Caroline, were raised there, but, sadly, my son-in-law, Randy, died in April of 2006 of a blood infection. Randy was a lovely man, and we all miss him terribly.

The rental house that we renovated in Redding now belongs to my son—he, his wife, and my grandson, Aaron, come out most weekends and stay there. They live in New York City, which is wonderfully close.

David started out as a musician; he went to Julliard through his master's degree. His major there was composing, and he worked in that field teaching and doing arrangements for a few years. Then he decided that was not a pathway that was going to work for him. At that point, he went back to graduate school at Columbia University to become a neuropsychologist. It's a specialty he has carved out, and he now has a very active private practice in New York City.

Amy continues a busy life in Redding and carries on Michael's lifelong interest and talent for relating to the animal world. This is in addition to having earned an MBA and being creatively gifted, especially in needlework. She has no horses now, but she currently shares her life with two bouncy border collies and an African Grey Parrot, the beautiful Ruby.

I am really proud of both my children, but let them write their own stories. They are both having wonderful, successful lives.

§

Now in Redding, I get to see that group of friends who began celebrating birthdays together nearly forty years ago, Bea and Arthur Shilstone and Mary Anne Guitar. Who knew back then at our round of fiftieth birthday parties, that we would all live this long? Last year, 2012, we all turned ninety! Being close to my lifelong friend, Polly Hathaway, has meant a great deal, too.

I've recently learned something, though perhaps I've known this all my life on some level. In an article I recently read, the author was using genetics, anthropology, psychology, and sociology to show the importance of our interconnectedness. It could be through family, friends, clients, colleagues, but regardless, these connections are what are most important and meaningful in life. I feel blessed and honored that I still have many connections in Redding, Connecticut; Athens, Georgia; and few other places. And above all, I feel wonderfully connected to my children and grandchildren.

A Life's Work

I do feel so blessed to have lived in this country through so many profound changes. As a child, I grew up surrounded by Kansas during the drought and the Great Depression. I then witnessed World War II from my post, which was so full of energy and creativity, then the civil rights movement and the women's movement, and now the digital age. I feel so lucky to have been part of each fascinating transformation, especially in this country, where it has always been possible to see hope and opportunity even in the hardest circumstances. My love of politics stemmed from this idealism, from the desire to support positive change. As we look to future changes, I will always be interested in how this country is governed and the principles that the government is based on.

I've also always been a people person—interested in connecting with people and interested in working in the helping professions. Maybe this focus is because of my father and mother. Even the work I did with the legislature in Connecticut was really driven by interacting with people. Then I was on the board of the Council on Aging in Athens for years and ran a caregiver-support group there. Finally, I did psychotherapy and counseling for all those years. So finding ways of connecting with people in a helpful way gives me a sense of satisfaction and motivates me politically and professionally. Even now I lead a caregivers' support group at Meadow Ridge, which is a modest way of continuing my life's work and following my favorite motto: "Do what you can, want what you have, be who you are."

I believe you have to look for the continuity in yourself, especially if you live a long time and experience a lot of changes in your life. Along with aging comes the need to connect the parts of yourself and integrate your life. The desire to make these connections then turns into the desire to make some kind of record. This project has been a way to do that: to review my life and leave some kind of record for my children, my grandchildren, and my friends.